FROM RUPEES TO RICHES: MASTER THE INDIAN WEALTH GAME

5 Exact Steps to Become a Millionaire If You Are in Your 20s or 30s

Leo K Yohan

Visualize Change

PROLOGUE

"From Rupees to Riches: Master the Indian Wealth Game" offers a compelling roadmap to achieving financial independence in your prime years. Tailored for the young and aspiring Indian, this book distills the essence of becoming a millionaire into 5 exact, actionable steps. Whether you're navigating the bustling cities or the serene countryside of India, this guide is your beacon through the complexities of the Indian economic landscape, promising strategies that resonate with your ambition to build wealth.

It's not just about financial growth; it's about molding a legacy of prosperity, wisdom, and impact. For those in their 20s and 30s, this book is a clarion call to action—your guide to transcending the ordinary and embarking on a journey of financial enlightenment, one strategic step at a time."

CONTENTS

Title Page
Prologue
Introduction
CHAPTER 1: The Assessment   1
CHAPTER 2: The Growth   10
CHAPTER 3: The Journey   16
CHAPTER 4: The Target   24
CHAPTER 5: The Extra Step   30
Epilogue   35

INTRODUCTION

A Journey to Financial Freedom in India

Imagine stepping into a realm where your financial aspirations aren't just fleeting daydreams but seeds of reality, waiting to sprout. This isn't a fairy tale; it's the vibrant, pulsating reality of modern India, a land of stark contrasts and boundless potential, where the dreams of becoming a millionaire in your 20s and 30s can indeed materialize, given the right mix of grit, wisdom, and strategy.

In this bustling nation, where tradition and innovation intertwine, the quest for financial independence is not just a personal goal; it's a clarion call for a generation poised on the edge of transformative change. The young Indians today are navigating a unique economic landscape, marked by the swift currents of technological advancement, a burgeoning startup ecosystem, and an evolving job market that demands adaptability and foresight.

The Indian Economic Canvas

India's economy, a kaleidoscope of traditional industries and digital innovations, offers a fertile ground for those daring enough to dream big. The startup scene, vibrant and burgeoning, has put India on the global map, signaling a shift from traditional employment to entrepreneurial ventures that tap into the digital economy's vast potential. This landscape is ripe with opportunities for the youth to leverage their skills, harness the power of technology, and carve out niches that resonate with a global audience.

Yet, this journey is not without its hurdles. Economic fluctuations, competitive pressures, and the ever-looming shadow of societal expectations create a complex maze that the aspiring millionaire must navigate. The path to financial freedom is fraught with challenges that test one's resolve, adaptability, and resilience.

The Call of the Millennials and Gen Z

The protagonists of this narrative, the Millennials and Gen Z, are not content to tread the beaten path. Armed with digital savvy, a global perspective, and an intrinsic desire for autonomy, they seek to redefine success. These are individuals who envision a life not confined by the nine-to-five grind but enriched by experiences, freedom, and the ability to make an impact.

This is where the journey diverges, splitting into countless paths, each marked by personal aspirations, skills, and the unyielding quest for growth. The road to financial independence in India is as diverse as its travelers, with each route offering lessons in resilience, creativity, and the art of possibility.

Stories of Transformation

Amidst the cacophony of the digital age, stories of individual transformation shine as beacons of inspiration. Consider the tale of a young woman from a small town who, armed with a laptop and an internet connection, builds a digital marketing empire that spans continents. Or the story of a college dropout who, through sheer tenacity and a knack for coding, launches a tech startup that revolutionizes the way rural India accesses healthcare.

These stories are not outliers but signposts of what's possible when ambition meets action. They underscore a fundamental truth: the journey to a million isn't paved with luck but with strategic moves, informed decisions, and an unwavering commitment to growth.

The Power of a Growth Mindset

At the heart of this journey lies the power of mindset. Financial literacy, once a neglected aspect of education, emerges as a critical tool for empowerment. Understanding the basics of budgeting, investing, and wealth management is not just practical; it's transformative. It equips the young dreamer with the knowledge to make informed decisions, to distinguish between fleeting trends and genuine opportunities, and to navigate the complexities of the financial world with confidence.

This book aims to demystify the process of wealth creation. It breaks down the journey into actionable steps, beginning with a deep dive into personal finance management, exploring avenues for growth and investment, and culminating in the art of sustaining and expanding one's wealth.

Laying the Foundation

The first step on this journey is introspection. A thorough assessment of one's financial health, skills, and aspirations sets the stage for targeted growth. It's about identifying your starting point, acknowledging your strengths, and pinpointing areas for development. This foundational step is crucial; it determines the direction of your journey and the strategies you'll employ to navigate the path ahead.

Envisioning the Future

Visualizing your future self is not just an exercise in daydreaming; it's a potent tool for motivation. It involves setting clear, achievable goals and mapping out a path to reach them. Whether it's achieving financial independence, creating a business that reflects your values, or building a portfolio that allows for early retirement, the clarity of your vision determines the solidity of your plan.

Commitment to the Journey

Embarking on this journey requires more than just a desire for wealth; it demands a commitment to continuous learning, adaptability, and discipline. The landscape of financial opportunities in India is constantly evolving, and staying ahead means being willing to learn new skills, adapt to changes, and embrace the latest technologies and trends.

The commitment also means being ready to face setbacks and failures head-on. The path to financial freedom is rarely linear. It's filled with obstacles, unexpected turns, and lessons that are only learned through experience. Embracing these challenges as opportunities for growth is what separates those who dream from those who achieve.

The Importance of Community and Mentorship

No journey is undertaken alone, and the quest for financial independence is no exception. The role of mentorship and community cannot be overstated. Connecting with individuals who have navigated their own paths to success provides invaluable insights and guidance. These relationships offer support, encourage accountability, and can open doors to opportunities that might otherwise remain hidden.

Furthermore, building a community of like-minded individuals creates a network of potential collaborators, partners, and supporters. It's a space for sharing knowledge, resources, and encouragement, making the journey not just more manageable, but also more fulfilling.

Strategies for Wealth Creation

This book will delve into the strategies that can accelerate the journey to financial freedom. From smart investing in stocks, real estate, and mutual funds to leveraging the gig economy for additional income streams, we'll explore the myriad ways to build and grow wealth. Understanding the principles of compound interest, risk management, and portfolio diversification will be key.

We'll also discuss the importance of creating passive income streams that can provide financial security and freedom. The goal is to make your money work for you, not the other way around. This includes looking into new-age investment opportunities such as cryptocurrencies and fintech innovations, which are rapidly transforming the financial landscape of India.

Sustainable Wealth Management

Finally, the journey to becoming a millionaire is not just about accumulating wealth; it's about managing it wisely and sustainably. This involves planning for the future, including retirement, estate planning, and wealth transfer. It also means considering the impact of your financial decisions on the broader community and the planet. Ethical investing, social entrepreneurship, and philanthropy are avenues through which your wealth can contribute to positive change in the world.

The Invitation

As we stand on the precipice of this journey, the path before us is clear. The journey to financial freedom in India, while challenging, is filled with opportunities for growth, impact, and fulfillment. This book is more than just a guide; it's an invitation to embark on a journey of transformation. It's an opportunity to redefine what success means to you and to take control of your financial future.

The steps outlined in the coming chapters are not merely theoretical; they are actionable and proven strategies that have led countless individuals to achieve their dreams of financial independence. Whether you're just starting out in your career, looking to pivot, or seeking ways to maximize your income and impact, the journey begins with a single step.

Let this book be your companion on the path to becoming a millionaire in India. With determination, strategy, and a willingness to learn and adapt, your financial dreams can become your reality. The journey starts now. Are you ready to take the first step?

CHAPTER 1: THE ASSESSMENT

Unlock Your Financial Snapshot

In the labyrinth of financial freedom, understanding where you stand is the key to finding your treasure. It's not just peering into your wallet or checking the bank balance; it's about unraveling the tapestry of your financial life—every thread from fixed deposits to mutual funds, salary to real estate, and beyond. Let's embark on this journey of self-discovery, mapping out your financial landscape in the vivid context of India's unique investment avenues and income streams.

The Fabric of Your Finances

Imagine your financial life as a vibrant fabric woven from various threads—each thread representing a different aspect of your finances. Some threads are bright and strong, symbolizing your assets and income streams, like salary, real estate, and hereditary assets. Other threads are more subdued, representing liabilities and expenditures. The goal is to understand this intricate weave, identifying areas of strength and those in need of mending.

Salary: The Steady Thread

For most, salary is the foundational thread in their financial fabric. It's steady, predictable, and often the primary source of income. But it's also where many stop weaving their financial destiny. In India, with its competitive job market and diverse economic sectors, understanding your market value is crucial. Are you being compensated fairly? Could upskilling or a job switch weave a stronger, brighter thread into your financial tapestry?

Fixed Deposits: The Traditional Safety Net

Fixed deposits (FDs) have long been the go-to for Indian savers. They're like the sturdy, reliable knots that secure the ends of your financial fabric. But in an era of fluctuating interest rates, the real value of money parked in FDs can unravel over time due to inflation. It's essential to assess how much of your wealth is tied up in FDs and whether these funds could be better deployed to weave a richer tapestry.

Mutual Funds: The Kaleidoscope of Opportunities

Mutual funds offer a spectrum of opportunities to diversify your financial fabric. They allow you to invest in a variety of sectors and asset classes, from the stability of debt funds to the vibrant potential of equity funds. The key is to understand your risk appetite and investment horizon. With Systematic Investment Plans (SIPs), even a modest thread of your monthly salary can be woven into a colorful pattern of long-term wealth.

Real Estate: The Cornerstone Block

Real estate in India is not just an asset; it's a cultural cornerstone. Whether it's the inherited family home or a strategic investment property, real estate adds both weight and warmth to your financial fabric. However, it's vital to assess these assets critically. Are they yielding the returns you expect? Is the emotional value overshadowing the financial utility? Real estate can be a golden thread in your fabric, but only if woven wisely.

Hereditary Assets: The Legacy Threads

Hereditary assets are the threads passed down through generations, imbued with emotional value and financial potential. In India, these can range from gold and jewelry to land and businesses. Assessing their current market value and potential growth is essential. Sometimes, repurposing these legacy threads can strengthen your financial fabric in ways you hadn't imagined.

Provident Fund & NPS: The Retirement Weave

The Employees' Provident Fund (EPF) and National Pension System (NPS) are the government's way of adding resilience to your financial fabric, ensuring it doesn't fray in your golden years. While these might seem like distant concerns, understanding their role and maximizing your contributions can add significant strength to your financial security. It's about seeing these not just as deductions from your salary, but as crucial weaves in your retirement tapestry.

Stocks: The Vibrant Risk-Reward Pattern

Investing in stocks can add vibrant, dynamic patterns to your financial fabric, offering high reward potential at a higher risk. The Indian stock market, with its array of sectors and companies, from burgeoning startups to established conglomerates, presents a landscape rich with opportunity. Educating yourself on stock market basics, staying informed about market trends, and perhaps even engaging a financial advisor can help you weave this thread with confidence.

As you navigate through the assessment of your financial landscape, delving deep into your assets reveals only one side of the tapestry. Equally critical is the examination of your liabilities, income streams, and expenditures. This holistic view forms the crux of creating a robust financial map, guiding you through the intricate maze of personal finance with clarity and purpose.

Assessing Liabilities: The Weights on Your Financial Fabric

Liabilities, the obligations and debts you owe, can weigh down your financial fabric, pulling tightly on its threads. In the Indian context, this might include home loans, car loans, personal loans, and credit card debt. Assessing your liabilities means not just listing them but understanding their terms—interest rates, repayment periods, and how they fit into your overall financial plan. Are these liabilities serving a purpose, helping you weave a stronger fabric, such as a home loan for a property that appreciates in value? Or are they unnecessary weights, like high-interest personal loans that could be consolidated or paid off to free up your financial weave?

Income Streams and Expenditures: The Flow of Your Financial Fabric

Your income streams extend beyond your primary salary. They may include part-time work, freelance projects, rental income from real estate, dividends from stocks, or returns from mutual funds and other investments. In the diverse economic landscape of India, recognizing and optimizing these streams can significantly enrich your financial fabric.

Expenditures, on the other hand, are the cuts made to your fabric. They range from necessary expenses, such as housing, utilities, and groceries, to discretionary spending on travel, dining, and entertainment. By mapping out your expenditures, you identify areas where the fabric may be fraying—where expenses can be trimmed or managed more efficiently to ensure a healthier financial state.

Securing Your Financial Foundation with Insurance

Once you have a clear understanding of your assets, liabilities, and the opportunities for growth, it's crucial to address the protection of your financial journey. Insurance stands as a sentinel, guarding against unforeseen events that could derail your progress. In India, where the landscape of financial security is as diverse as its culture, understanding and selecting the right insurance policies become indispensable.

Types of Insurance to Consider:

Health Insurance: With healthcare costs rising, a comprehensive health insurance policy ensures you and your family are protected against hefty medical bills, allowing you to preserve your savings for future goals.

Life Insurance: Life insurance is essential, especially if you have dependents. It provides financial security to your loved ones in your absence, ensuring their financial goals and daily needs are taken care of.

Property and Casualty Insurance: Protecting your physical assets, such as your home and vehicle, against damage or loss, is crucial. These policies safeguard your investment in these assets, ensuring you're not left financially vulnerable.

Liability Insurance: In a world of uncertainties, liability insurance protects you against claims resulting from injuries and damage to people or property, an often overlooked aspect of comprehensive financial planning.

Incorporating Insurance into Your Financial Plan

Incorporating insurance into your financial plan is not just about mitigating risks; it's about ensuring continuity and stability in your wealth-building journey. Review your insurance coverage regularly to adjust for life changes, such as marriage, parenthood, or purchasing a home, to ensure your coverage matches your evolving needs.

By securing a robust insurance framework, you fortify your financial structure against the storms of life, ensuring that when challenges arise, your path to financial freedom remains unobstructed.

Creating Your Financial Map: Charting the Path Ahead

With a comprehensive understanding of your assets, liabilities, income streams, and expenditures, you're now equipped to create your financial map. This isn't merely a budget but a dynamic tool that reflects your current financial situation and guides your future decisions. In the context of India's evolving financial environment, this map should be adaptable, allowing for adjustments as your financial landscape changes.

Utilize spreadsheets or personal finance apps designed for the Indian market to track and visualize your finances. These tools can help you set goals, such as paying off debt, saving for a down payment on a property, or investing in mutual funds or stocks. They also allow you to monitor your progress, adjust your strategies, and stay on course towards your financial objectives.

Empowering Your Journey with Knowledge and Action

Understanding the flow of your income and expenditures, alongside a clear view of your assets and liabilities, empowers you to make informed decisions. It highlights the importance of financial literacy in navigating India's unique economic opportunities and challenges. This chapter has laid the groundwork for your financial enlightenment, equipping you with the tools to assess your current position accurately and to chart a course for growth and prosperity.

The Road Ahead

As we move forward from this assessment, remember, the ultimate goal is not just to admire the complexity and beauty of your financial tapestry as it stands today, but to actively design and weave the future you envision. Your financial map is not static; it's a living, evolving representation of your financial journey.

Adjusting Your Loom

With your financial snapshot laid bare, the next steps involve adjusting your strategies to better align with your goals. Perhaps you'll find that reallocating resources from traditional fixed deposits to more dynamic mutual funds can enhance your fabric's overall pattern. Or you might discover that the emotional weight of hereditary assets is holding back their financial potential, prompting a reevaluation of their place in your portfolio.

The Strategy of Diversification

Diversification is akin to introducing a multitude of colors and patterns into your fabric, enhancing its resilience and beauty. Just as a weaver selects threads to create a harmonious design, you must choose your investments to build a balanced and diversified financial portfolio. This means spreading your investments across different asset classes (stocks, real estate, mutual funds) and within asset classes (diverse sectors, SIPs in different mutual funds), to mitigate risk and optimize returns.

Leveraging Technology

In today's digital age, numerous tools and platforms can help you assess and manage your finances more effectively. From online calculators for mutual funds and NPS to apps that track stock performance and real estate trends, leveraging technology can provide you with real-time insights and data-driven strategies to fortify your financial fabric.

Education and Continuous Learning

The landscape of personal finance, especially in a rapidly evolving economy like India's, is constantly changing. Staying informed through financial news, subscribing to investment blogs, attending workshops, and even considering courses on financial planning can enrich your knowledge. This ongoing education is not just about making informed decisions today but about staying adaptable and proactive in the face of future financial challenges and opportunities.

Seeking Professional Advice

Sometimes, the best way to understand the intricate patterns of your financial fabric is to seek the perspective of a skilled artisan —or in this case, a financial advisor. A professional can offer personalized advice tailored to your financial situation, helping you identify areas for growth, strategies for risk management, and opportunities you may have overlooked. In the complex world of finance, a trusted advisor can be an invaluable resource.

Empowering Your Financial Journey

The assessment you've embarked upon is more than an exercise in financial introspection; it's the first step on a path to empowerment. By understanding where you stand, you lay the groundwork for where you wish to go. Your financial dreams, whether they involve buying a home, securing your retirement, or achieving true financial independence, all start with this foundational knowledge.

As you conclude this first chapter of your financial journey, remember that the map you've laid out is not just a reflection of your current state but a blueprint for your future. Each thread of your financial fabric, from the stability of fixed deposits and provident funds to the dynamic potential of stocks and mutual funds, plays a crucial role in the tapestry of your financial future.

In the coming chapters, we'll explore how to build upon this foundation, weaving new threads and patterns into your financial fabric to create a masterpiece of personal wealth and freedom. The journey to financial independence in India is as diverse as its people, and with the right knowledge, strategies, and actions, your financial dreams can become a vivid reality.

CHAPTER 2: THE GROWTH

Elevate Your Game

As the dawn breaks over the bustling cities and serene villages of India, a new era of opportunity is awakening. In this chapter, we embark on a journey not just of financial growth but of personal and professional evolution. The landscape of India's economy, with its dynamic blend of tradition and innovation, presents a fertile ground for those willing to cultivate their potential. Here, amidst the tech hubs of Bangalore and the financial districts of Mumbai, through the green energy projects dotting rural landscapes, lies your path to growth.

Navigating India's Economic Renaissance

India's economy is a tapestry rich with opportunities, woven from threads of technological advancement, financial innovation, and sustainable development. Each sector, from the pulsating world of IT to the transformative realms of fintech and green energy, offers unique pathways to success.

The key to navigating this complex landscape is understanding the macroeconomic trends and aligning your career trajectory with industries poised for growth. Reports from NASSCOM and the Ministry of New and Renewable Energy offer insights into burgeoning sectors, while financial newspapers and magazines provide analysis on market dynamics. Dive deep into this wealth of information, identifying where your passion intersects with opportunity.

Cultivating High-Demand Skills

In the soil of opportunity, it's the seeds of skill that you sow which will determine the harvest of your success. India's economic growth is increasingly powered by technology, making digital literacy not just an asset but a necessity. Skills in AI, machine learning, blockchain, and cybersecurity are in high demand, as are expertise in digital marketing and product management within the fintech sector.

Equally, the push towards sustainable energy sources has spiked demand for professionals in green technology and environmental science. The Indian government's commitment to renewable energy targets spells abundant opportunities for innovation and entrepreneurship in this sector.

Yet, acquiring skills is just the beginning. The true growth lies in applying them creatively to solve real-world problems. Engage in projects, internships, or start-ups that allow you to put your skills to the test, challenging you to learn, adapt, and innovate.

The Art and Science of Networking

In the vibrant markets and online forums of India, networking emerges as a vital bridge to opportunities. It's an art that involves more than just making connections; it's about nurturing relationships, exchanging value, and building a web of contacts that can support your growth journey.

Attend industry meetups, seminars, and conferences to connect with peers and industry leaders. Engage actively on professional networking sites like LinkedIn, sharing your insights and work, commenting on discussions, and connecting with professionals in your field of interest. Remember, effective networking is reciprocal; always look for ways to contribute to your network, offering help, advice, or connections where you can.

The Transformative Power of Mentorship

Mentorship can be a beacon of guidance in the complex journey of career growth. A mentor offers not just advice but wisdom, drawn from their experiences and mistakes. In India, where the professional landscape can often be nuanced and challenging to navigate, a mentor can help steer you towards your goals, opening doors to opportunities and providing insights that can leapfrog your growth.

Finding a mentor requires initiative and sincerity. Identify professionals whose career paths resonate with your aspirations. Reach out with thoughtful questions or requests for guidance, showing appreciation for their time and expertise. A successful mentorship relationship is built on mutual respect and learning; be open to feedback and willing to put in the work to grow.

Embracing a Growth Mindset

The cornerstone of your journey in this chapter and beyond is the growth mindset—the unwavering belief in your ability to learn, grow, and improve. This mindset is your compass in navigating the challenges and opportunities of India's economic landscape. It drives you to seek out new knowledge, to persevere through setbacks, and to view every experience as a step toward your ultimate goal of financial independence.

This mindset is particularly crucial in a country like India, where rapid changes in technology, economy, and society require adaptability and lifelong learning. Embrace the challenges as opportunities to stretch your abilities and expand your horizons.

Leveraging Technology for Growth

In today's digital age, technology is not just a sector to work in but a tool to accelerate your growth. Online platforms offer unprecedented access to learning resources, industry insights, and networking opportunities. Use these tools to stay ahead of the curve, keeping abreast of new developments in your field, enhancing your skills, and connecting with thought leaders and potential mentors.

Building Your Personal Brand

In the crowded professional landscape of India, standing out requires more than just skill and ambition—it demands a personal brand that resonates with your professional ethos and aspirations. Your personal brand is the narrative you weave about your career journey, skills, accomplishments, and goals. It's how you present yourself in professional settings, both online and offline, distinguishing you from your peers.

Crafting this brand involves several key strategies:

- Consistency Across Platforms: Ensure that your LinkedIn, Twitter, and any professional blogs or websites present a coherent image of your professional interests and achievements.

- Value-Driven Content: Share insights, write articles, or contribute to discussions in your field of expertise. This not only showcases your knowledge but also demonstrates your commitment to adding value to your community.

- Engagement: Engaging with industry leaders, participating in relevant conversations, and offering your perspective can elevate your visibility and establish you as a thought leader in your domain.

Fostering Innovation and Entrepreneurship

India's economic landscape is fertile ground for entrepreneurs and innovators. With the government's support for startups through initiatives like Startup India, and the growing investor interest in innovative business models, the environment has never been more conducive for entrepreneurship.

Whether it's leveraging technology to address societal challenges, creating sustainable solutions for India's growing energy needs, or innovating in the fintech space to make financial services more accessible, the opportunities for growth through entrepreneurship are vast. However, entrepreneurship requires more than just a great idea; it demands resilience, strategic planning, and the ability to pivot and adapt to market feedback.

Strategic Planning and Goal Setting

Growth is not a product of chance; it's the result of strategic planning and relentless execution. Set clear, measurable goals for your career growth, identifying both short-term milestones and long-term objectives. Align your learning, networking, and professional activities to support these goals, and regularly review your progress, adjusting your strategy as needed.

In the dynamic context of India's economy, staying agile and open to new directions can uncover opportunities you hadn't initially considered. It may mean shifting industries, acquiring new skills, or even starting a venture of your own.

Lifelong Learning as a Lifestyle

Adopting lifelong learning as a lifestyle is crucial for sustained growth in the modern workforce, especially in a rapidly developing country like India. The learning doesn't stop with formal education; it continues through professional experiences, self-study, online courses, workshops, and beyond.

The pursuit of knowledge not only enhances your skill set but also fosters a curious, adaptable mindset that can navigate the complexities of India's economic and professional landscape. It prepares you to seize opportunities in emerging fields and to tackle challenges with innovative solutions.

The journey of growth in India's unique economic and professional landscape is both challenging and exhilarating. By focusing on high-demand skills and industries, leveraging the power of networking, seeking mentorship, and nurturing a growth mindset, you set the stage for a fulfilling career that not only meets but exceeds your financial goals.

Remember, growth is a continuous process, a journey that requires patience, perseverance, and a proactive approach to learning and development. With the strategies outlined in this chapter, you are well-equipped to elevate your game, harnessing India's vibrant economic opportunities to build a prosperous, rewarding future.

CHAPTER 3: THE JOURNEY

Strategize Your Wealth

As we turn the pages from understanding and growth to the heart of your financial journey—strategy—it's time to sculpt the blueprint of your wealth with precision and care. Here, in the bustling markets and digital finance platforms of India, your financial acumen is put to the test. It's where budgeting isn't just tracking expenses but crafting a vision for your future, where investing transcends saving to become a cornerstone of wealth creation, and where side hustles are not merely gigs but gateways to financial independence. This chapter is your guide through the intricate dance of strategizing your wealth, ensuring every rupee you earn not only counts but multiplies.

Budgeting Like a Pro

In the vibrant economic tapestry of India, budgeting is the art of balancing your dreams with reality. It's understanding that each expenditure holds the potential to either inch you closer to your goals or pull you away. Start with a clear outline of your income and expenses, employing tools and apps designed with the Indian market in mind to track your financial flow.

But true budgeting mastery lies in prioritizing. Assign your income to categories using the 50/30/20 rule—50% on necessities, 30% on wants, and 20% into savings and investments. Yet, in India's context, flexibility is key. With rising costs and fluctuating incomes, adjusting these percentages to fit your reality can make all the difference. Remember, a budget is not a constraint but a liberator, providing the freedom to enjoy today while securing tomorrow.

Investing Wisely in the Indian Market

Investing in India offers a kaleidoscope of opportunities, each with its unique flavor and potential. The stock market, with its allure of high returns, demands a blend of patience, research, and resilience. Start with understanding the basics of the Bombay Stock Exchange (BSE) and National Stock Exchange (NSE), and use mutual funds as a vehicle to diversify your investment across a spectrum of assets.

Yet, the Indian market's charm isn't limited to stocks. Real estate, despite its challenges, remains a favored asset, promising not just returns but security. Investing in property requires a keen eye on location, legalities, and market trends, ensuring that your investment grows as India's urban landscapes flourish.

For those looking beyond traditional avenues, the Indian market is ripe with alternative investments. Commodities, gold, and government schemes like the Public Provident Fund (PPF) offer avenues for diversification. The key is to align your investment choices with your financial goals, risk tolerance, and the horizon of your investment journey.

Mastering the Consistency Game

In the realm of wealth creation, consistency is your most potent ally. It's the discipline to stick to your budget, the commitment to regularly invest, and the perseverance to grow your side hustle, even when the going gets tough. In India, where economic conditions can swiftly change, this consistency is what separates the successful from the wishful thinkers.

Automate your savings and investments wherever possible, taking advantage of India's growing fintech solutions. SIPs (Systematic Investment Plans) in mutual funds, automatic transfers to savings accounts, and recurring deposits are tools that help maintain your investment rhythm without the need for daily oversight.

Exploring Side Hustles

In today's digital age, the Indian economy is a fertile ground for side hustles. With the internet erasing geographical barriers, opportunities to earn extra income are vast. From freelance writing and digital marketing to online tutoring and e-commerce, the gig economy is booming.

Yet, the true essence of a successful side hustle lies in leveraging your unique skills and passions. It's about identifying a niche that not only brings in extra income but also enriches your professional and personal life. Whether it's starting a YouTube channel to share your expertise or creating an online course, your side hustle can be a powerful vehicle for achieving financial goals sooner than anticipated.

Navigating Taxes and Regulations

Understanding the tax implications of your investments and side hustles is crucial in the Indian context. Efficient tax planning can significantly enhance your returns, making it an integral part of your wealth strategy. Familiarize yourself with the tax benefits of various investment vehicles, from the tax-saving advantages of ELSS mutual funds to the exemptions on long-term capital gains in stocks and real estate.

For your side hustle, keeping meticulous records and understanding the GST implications can save you from future headaches. Consider consulting a tax professional to navigate the complexities of India's tax landscape, ensuring that your efforts to grow your wealth are not eroded by unforeseen tax liabilities.

Creating a Comprehensive Wealth Strategy

A comprehensive wealth strategy in India's dynamic economic landscape is akin to navigating a river's currents—knowing when to paddle hard and when to let the flow guide you. It combines the rigor of budgeting, the foresight of investing, and the innovation of side hustles, all while navigating the nuances of tax regulations. This strategy isn't static; it evolves as you move closer to your goals, reflecting the changing economic environment, your personal growth, and shifts in your financial priorities.

The Pillars of a Solid Strategy

Holistic Planning: Your wealth strategy should encompass all aspects of your financial life—from daily expenses, insurances and emergency funds to long-term investments and retirement planning. Each decision you make should fit into this broader framework, ensuring that short-term actions align with long-term objectives.

Risk Management: Understanding and managing risk is paramount. Diversification across asset classes and sectors mitigates risk, providing a safety net against market volatility. In India's diverse market, balancing between equities, fixed income, real estate, and alternative investments can help safeguard your portfolio.

Regular Reviews and Adjustments: The economic landscape in India is dynamic, influenced by global trends, government policies, and market sentiment. Regularly reviewing your financial plan allows you to adapt to these changes, optimizing your strategy to capture new opportunities or mitigate emerging risks.

Financial Discipline: Perhaps the most challenging yet rewarding aspect of your strategy is maintaining financial discipline. This means sticking to your budget, consistently investing according to your plan, and resisting the temptation to divert from your strategy based on short-term market movements or speculative opportunities.

A Practical Illustration: The Power of Index Funds

Consider the journey of Rohit, a 30-year-old software engineer from Pune. Like many, Rohit dreams of financial independence but feels overwhelmed by the myriad investment options available. After researching and consulting with a financial advisor, he decides to embark on a path of consistent investment in an index fund, attracted by the blend of diversification and the historical performance of the Indian stock market.

Rohit's Strategy:

Rohit commits to investing ₹40,000 monthly in a well-regarded index fund that tracks the NIFTY 50, an index representing the performance of 50 large, well-established companies listed on the National Stock Exchange of India. This index fund offers a diversified portfolio in itself, mitigating risk while allowing Rohit to partake in the growth of India's economy.

The Magic of Compounding:

Assuming an average annual return of 12%—a reasonable expectation based on the historical performance of the Indian stock market—let's break down the numbers to see how Rohit's investment grows over 25 years:

- Monthly Investment: ₹40,000

- Investment Period: 25 years
- Expected Annual Return: 12%

Using the formula for calculating the future value of a series of investments (an annuity), we can estimate the growth of Rohit's investment over the 25 years.

Let's calculate the future value of Rohit's investment.

$$\text{Future Value} = P \times \left(\frac{(1+r)^n - 1}{r}\right)$$

where:
- P is the monthly investment (₹40,000)
- r is the monthly interest rate (12% annual interest rate converted to monthly, which is 1% or 0.01 as a decimal)
- n is the total number of payments (300 months for 25 years).

Let's compute the future value to see the outcome of Rohit's investment strategy.

Rohit's disciplined monthly investment of ₹40,000 in an index fund, assuming an average annual return of 12%, would grow to approximately ₹7.5 crore over 25 years. This example showcases the transformative power of consistent investing and compound interest, illustrating how a strategic approach to wealth can turn the dream of financial independence into a tangible reality.

Key Takeaways:

- Start Early: The earlier you begin investing, the more time your money has to compound and grow.
- Stay Consistent: Regular, disciplined investments can lead to substantial wealth accumulation over time.
- Understand the Power of Compounding: Compounding

interest allows your investments to generate earnings, which are then reinvested to generate their own earnings, leading to exponential growth over the long term.

Rohit's story is a compelling illustration of how embracing a strategic approach to investing, centered around consistency and the power of the market's growth, can significantly impact your financial future. It underscores the importance of making informed, disciplined financial decisions, providing a roadmap for readers looking to navigate the journey towards financial independence in India.

Leveraging Technology for Financial Empowerment

In today's digital era, technology plays a crucial role in strategizing your wealth. From budgeting apps and online investment platforms to tax planning tools, leveraging technology can streamline your financial management, offering insights and efficiencies that were previously out of reach. In the context of India, with its rapidly growing fintech sector, these tools are increasingly accessible, providing customized solutions suited to the Indian market and regulatory environment.

The Role of Professional Advice

As you navigate the complexities of creating and executing a wealth strategy, professional advice can be invaluable. Financial advisors, tax consultants, and investment professionals offer expertise that can enhance your strategy's effectiveness, tailor-made for your personal circumstances and goals. In India, where personal finance can sometimes seem daunting, these professionals can demystify the process, guiding you through the intricacies of investment options, tax planning, and regulatory compliance.

Embracing the Journey

Strategizing your wealth is more than a set of financial actions; it's a journey of personal and financial growth. It requires patience, resilience, and a proactive approach to learning and adaptation. Celebrate the milestones along the way, learn from the setbacks, and remain focused on your vision of financial freedom.

In India, a country of vast economic diversity and opportunity, this journey holds the promise of not just financial security but also the fulfillment of your potential and aspirations. Your strategy, informed by insight and executed with determination, paves the way for a future where your finances serve not as a source of stress but as a foundation for achieving your dreams.

CHAPTER 4: THE TARGET

Set Milestones, Achieve Goals

Imagine embarking on a trek through the majestic Himalayas. Your ultimate summit? The elusive millionaire status. But the path isn't just a straight climb. It weaves through valleys and peaks, demanding not just strength but strategy. In this adventure, your milestones are your base camps—essential markers that guide your ascent, offering rest, reflection, and redirection. This chapter is your map and compass, designed to navigate the financial highlands with precision and purpose.

The Art of Setting Milestones - The Blueprint of Dreams

Begin by drafting a blueprint of your financial dreams. These aren't mere daydreams but visions of what you truly aspire to achieve: a house in a serene locality, a fund for your children's education, travel to distant lands, or the peace of early retirement. Break these dreams down into achievable milestones. Similar to plotting points on a map, these milestones are your markers of progress, your indicators of success.

Setting milestones begins with envisioning your summit—financial independence. Break down this ultimate goal into achievable camps. Think of them as short (1-3 years), medium (3-5 years), and long-term (5+ years) objectives. These might include saving for a down payment on a home, reaching a specific net worth, or generating a target passive income stream.

- Short-Term Milestones: Could be clearing credit card debt or building an emergency fund worth six months of expenses. These are your initial camps, ensuring you're prepared for the journey ahead.
- Medium-Term Milestones: Might involve acquiring an investment property or maximizing your retirement fund contributions. These camps push you closer to the peak, offering clearer views of your financial landscape.
- Long-Term Milestones: Here lies the summit—achieving a net worth that grants you the title of a millionaire, with diversified investments and sustainable income sources lighting up the path.

Let's try to elaborate these milestones systematically.

Milestone 1: Understanding Your Financial Baseline

Before you embark on this journey, take a moment to assess where you stand. Just as a marathoner needs to know their current fitness level to plan their training, understanding your financial baseline is crucial. This involves calculating your net worth—subtracting your liabilities from your assets—to get a clear picture of your starting point.

Milestone 2: Building an Emergency Fund

An essential early milestone is establishing an emergency fund, a financial buffer to protect you against life's unforeseen challenges. Aim to save at least six months' worth of living expenses. This fund ensures that unexpected events—a job loss, a medical emergency—don't derail your long-term financial goals.

Milestone 3: Debt Reduction

In the pursuit of financial independence, high-interest debt is a significant hurdle. Set a milestone to pay off such debts, starting with those carrying the highest interest rates. Use strategies like the snowball or avalanche method to systematically reduce and eventually eliminate debt.

Milestone 4: Consistent Investment

Investing is the vehicle that accelerates your journey to wealth. A key milestone is establishing a regular investment habit. Leveraging the example from the previous chapter, committing a fixed amount monthly to investments like index funds can significantly compound your wealth over time. Tailor this milestone to match your risk tolerance and investment horizon, exploring diverse options within the Indian market—from equities to real estate, mutual funds to government schemes.

Milestone 5: Diversification and Portfolio Review

Diversification is your safeguard against market volatility. Set a milestone to review and diversify your investment portfolio regularly. This could involve rebalancing your asset allocation or exploring new investment avenues as you gain more confidence and understanding of the market.

Milestone 6: Education and Skill Enhancement

Investing in yourself is equally important. A milestone dedicated to acquiring new skills or advancing your education can open doors to higher earning potential and career advancement, further fueling your journey to financial independence.

Crafting Your Route - Your Progress

With your base camps mapped, it's time to chart your route. Each milestone requires a unique strategy—blending aggressive saving, smart investing, and perhaps side hustles. Tools and apps designed for the Indian financial landscape can be your guides, tracking expenses, investments, and progress towards each milestone.

But the journey is as unpredictable as the weather in the Himalayas. Flexibility is key. Regularly review your plan, adapting to changes in your personal life, the economy, or financial goals. Just as a seasoned climber knows when to push forward or seek shelter, knowing when to adjust your financial strategies is crucial.

The Trekking Gear: Budgets and Tools

Your budget is your trekking gear, essential for the journey. It's not just about limiting expenses; it's about maximizing your resources—allocating funds towards savings, investments, and debt repayment efficiently. Pair your budget with the right tools—investment calculators, budgeting apps, and financial planning software specifically catered to the Indian market. These tools not only help track your progress but also offer insights to optimize your route.

Staying Motivated on the Ascent

The path to your financial summit is fraught with challenges—market downturns, unexpected expenses, or moments of doubt. Here, the stories of those who've reached their summits can inspire. Engage with communities, online forums, or financial blogs where people share their journeys. Learn from their struggles and triumphs.

The path to financial independence, much like a marathon, tests not just your physical endurance but your mental fortitude. Here are strategies to keep you motivated:

- Visualize Your Success: Regularly visualize achieving your milestones and ultimate goal. This mental imagery can be a

powerful motivator, keeping you focused and driven.
- **Celebrate Milestones:** Recognize and celebrate each milestone, no matter how small. These celebrations reinforce positive behavior and keep you motivated for the next leg of the journey.
- **Build a Support Network:** Surround yourself with like-minded individuals. Whether it's a financial advisor, a mentor, or a community of aspiring millionaires, a support network can provide encouragement, advice, and accountability.
- **Adapt and Learn:** Be prepared to adapt your strategy as you learn more about yourself and the market. Flexibility and a willingness to learn from both successes and setbacks are crucial in maintaining momentum.

It is very important to celebrate your own milestones, no matter how small. Each base camp reached is a testament to your discipline and dedication. These celebrations are not just rewards but reminders of the progress you've made, fueling your journey forward.

The Summit Awaits

As you advance from one milestone to the next, the summit becomes more than just a dream—it's a destination within reach. The discipline of setting clear targets, the adaptability to navigate the changing terrain, and the persistence to keep moving forward, transform your financial journey into an adventure of a lifetime.

Remember, the summit of financial independence isn't just about the view—it's about the person you become along the way. Each step, each milestone, crafts you into a more disciplined, knowledgeable, and resilient individual, capable of not just reaching but surpassing every peak you set your sights on.

In the end, the journey to a million isn't just a trek through the financial highlands. It's a voyage of self-discovery, with each milestone a marker of your growth, each challenge an opportunity to learn, and the summit a testament to your perseverance and strategy. So, lace up your boots, set your sights on the first base camp, and begin the ascent. The path to financial independence is steep, but for those willing to make the climb, the summit of success awaits.

CHAPTER 5: THE EXTRA STEP

Beyond the Basics

As you ascend the summit of your financial Everest, a breathtaking vista unfolds—not just of the path traversed but of the horizon yet to explore. This is where the narrative of wealth transcends the ledger, weaving into the fabric of society and the environment, crafting a legacy that resonates with purpose, ethics, and sustainability. Welcome to the chapter where your financial journey illuminates broader horizons—where your success becomes a beacon for ethical investing, philanthropy, and the stewardship of a sustainable future.

The Beacon of Ethical Investing

Imagine your investments as seeds. Where you plant these seeds and how you nurture them can change the landscape of the future. Ethical investing is about choosing fertile grounds that promise not just financial returns but also contribute to a flourishing ecosystem. It's about investing in companies that are not merely profit-driven but are stewards of environmental care, champions of social responsibility, and advocates for good governance.

In the context of India's burgeoning economy, ethical investing could mean supporting clean energy initiatives that aim to power villages with sustainable sources, backing enterprises that champion fair labor practices, or investing in technologies that seek to solve pressing environmental challenges. Each investment decision is a vote for the kind of world you wish to live in and leave behind.

Philanthropy: The Harmony of Giving

Philanthropy in India is a rich tapestry, woven through with threads of tradition, culture, and an innate sense of community. It's about leveraging your financial success to compose a symphony of change, orchestrating opportunities that uplift and empower. This isn't just about monetary donations; it's about investing time, sharing knowledge, and mentoring the next generation.

Picture initiating a program that bridges the digital divide, offering young minds in remote areas access to the world's knowledge. Or envision founding a startup incubator that nurtures social enterprises addressing India's unique challenges. Your philanthropic efforts can spark movements, inspire others to contribute, and create a legacy of compassion and innovation.

Sustainable Wealth Management: Crafting a Future

Sustainable wealth management is akin to building a legacy house, one brick at a time, ensuring it stands strong for generations to come. It's a holistic approach that balances growth with sustainability, integrating ethical investments, philanthropy, and environmental stewardship into a cohesive wealth management strategy.

Consider the impact of setting up a family foundation focused on sustainability, creating a fund that supports environmental research, or establishing a scholarship for students in sustainable development. These actions not only ensure the longevity of your wealth but also its alignment with creating a positive impact on the world.

The Journey of Legacy Building

Building a legacy is an art. It's about painting a picture of the future with strokes of your values, beliefs, and hopes. This legacy transcends monetary wealth, encompassing the impact you make, the lives you touch, and the footprints you leave on the environment. It's about being remembered not just for what you had but for what you gave, what you stood for, and how you contributed to the welfare of the planet.

Imagine, years from now, a world where your investments have contributed to significant advancements in renewable energy, your philanthropic efforts have empowered thousands to lift themselves out of poverty, and your commitment to sustainability has inspired a movement towards more responsible living. This is the essence of a true legacy—one that creates ripples of positive change.

Engaging in the Circle of Impact

The journey to creating a lasting legacy is a collaborative endeavor. It involves engaging with communities, joining forces with like-minded individuals, and participating in or creating platforms for change. It's about sharing your journey, the lessons learned, the successes, and even the failures, to inspire and catalyze further action.

Platforms for impact investment, philanthropic networks, and sustainability forums are burgeoning, especially in India, offering avenues to amplify your efforts. By engaging in these circles, your journey towards creating a legacy becomes part of a larger narrative of collective impact, where every contribution, no matter the size, plays a crucial role in shaping the future.

The Symphony of Legacy

As this chapter—and your journey—nears its close, reflect on the symphony you've begun to compose. Each note represents a choice, an action, an investment in the future. The melody is yours to create, a harmonious blend of wealth, ethics, and impact. This isn't the end of your financial journey but a new beginning, where your wealth serves a purpose beyond the numbers, contributing to a legacy that endures.

Remember, the steps you take beyond the basics of accumulating wealth—towards ethical investing, philanthropy, and sustainable wealth management—craft a narrative of your life that's measured not by the wealth you amassed but by the impact you made and the legacy you leave behind. It's a narrative that echoes through the lives you've touched, the communities you've uplifted, and the environment you've preserved. This is the true power of wealth – its ability to create a positive, lasting change.

In the heart of India, where the spirit of giving and community is woven into the very fabric of society, your journey towards building a legacy is supported by a rich cultural heritage of philanthropy and stewardship. It's a journey that invites you to look beyond your individual aspirations, to see your wealth as a tool for broader societal and environmental good.

Crafting Your Legacy: A Call to Action

This chapter is more than just a guide; it's a call to action. It's an invitation to step into a role that few dare to embrace fully – that of a changemaker, a visionary, and a guardian of the future. Start small if you must, but start. Whether it's choosing to invest in a sustainable startup, volunteering your time and expertise to a cause, or simply making more informed, ethical financial decisions, every action counts.

Your legacy is defined not just by the wealth you accumulate but by how you choose to use that wealth. It's a testament to your values, your vision for the future, and your commitment to leaving the world a better place than you found it. In the vibrant, diverse, and rapidly changing landscape of India, the opportunities to make a meaningful impact are endless.

A Tapestry of Lives: The Ultimate Legacy

As you embark on this journey beyond the basics, remember that the ultimate legacy is a tapestry of lives changed, environments preserved, and societies transformed. It's about creating a story that inspires future generations to carry forward the torch of ethical stewardship, philanthropy, and sustainable growth.

Imagine, years from now, looking back on a journey that did more than just secure your financial freedom. A journey that sparked a movement, inspired a community, and built a legacy of positive impact. This is the promise of taking that extra step – of moving beyond the basics to truly harness the power of your wealth.

In the end, the journey to becoming a millionaire, to building wealth, is as much about the mark you leave on the world as it is about the milestones you achieve. It's a journey that challenges you to think bigger, act bolder, and dream beyond the confines of your own life. So, as you turn the pages of this chapter and look to the future, ask yourself: What legacy do I want to leave? How can I use my wealth to create a world that reflects my deepest values and highest aspirations?

This is your invitation to join a select group of individuals who understand that true wealth is measured not by what they have, but by what they give. It's your moment to take the extra step, to go beyond the basics, and to embark on the most rewarding journey of all – the journey of building a lasting legacy.

EPILOGUE

As we draw the curtains on this expedition, not of miles but of milestones, let's pause and breathe in the essence of our journey. This voyage was never just about the accumulation of wealth; it was a pilgrimage towards transformation—of self, of lives, and of narratives. The chapters you've journeyed through are not mere instructions; they are the melody of ambition, the rhythm of strategy, and the harmony of action, all coming together to compose the symphony of financial freedom.

Embracing the Transformation

Think of this not just as a conclusion but as a commencement—a threshold where dreams meet determination. These pages were designed to be more than a roadmap; they were meant to ignite a spark within you. A spark that, when fanned by the winds of action, can become a beacon guiding not just your path, but also illuminating the way for others.

The Beauty of the Journey

The path to financial independence is painted with the broad strokes of experiences, with each hue representing a lesson learned, a challenge overcome, or a victory celebrated. It's a canvas that reflects growth, resilience, and the sheer beauty of evolving.

Remember, the wealth you seek to accumulate is but a reflection of the wealth of experiences you gather along the way.

This journey towards creating lasting wealth is also a journey of legacy-building—a testament to the impact your wealth can wield, not just in numbers, but in the positive change it can spur in the world around you. It's about crafting a legacy that outlives bank statements, one that is measured in the smiles of those you've helped and the betterment of the communities you've uplifted.

Armed and Ready

Now, as you stand on the precipice of action, you are armed—not just with knowledge, but with a vision. You possess the strategies to navigate through the complexities of financial success in the vibrant tapestry that is India. This book was not a monologue, but a dialogue—a conversation between these pages and your aspirations.

Taking that leap might seem daunting, yet within you lies the courage and the blueprint to turn your millionaire dreams into your reality. It's a leap not into the unknown, but towards a future you've meticulously crafted with every word absorbed from this journey.

A Beacon of Possibility

Let this book serve not just as a guide, but as a lantern lighting up the path of possibility. It's a testament to the fact that your dreams of wealth and impact are not just feasible; they are within reach, waiting for your stride.

The road to becoming a millionaire is more than just a path of financial accrual; it's a road paved with the stones of persistence, knowledge, and intentional action. And now, it stretches before you, inviting you to embark.

Crafting Your Tomorrow

As you turn the final page of this chapter and look towards the horizon, remember, the future doesn't just happen—it's crafted. Every decision you make, every step you take, is a brushstroke on the canvas of tomorrow.

This journey you're on is about etching a story not just of financial success, but of a life rich with purpose, a spirit imbued with generosity, and actions resonant with impact. Your quest for financial freedom is a narrative in the making, a saga of transformation that transcends the personal to touch the lives of many.

So, take that step, embrace the journey, and embark on the most exhilarating adventure of all—the quest to turn your dreams into reality, one determined step at a time. The future isn't just yours for the taking; it's yours for the making. Let's not just chase those millionaire dreams; let's live them, one impactful, strategic, and ambitious step at a time.

The world is not just a stage but a canvas, and you, armed with the palette of possibilities this book offers, are ready to create your masterpiece. Let's make those millionaire dreams a reality, one step at a time. The future is yours to create, and the world is waiting to see what you will build with it.

www.ingramcontent.com/pod-product-compliance
Lightning Source LLC
Chambersburg PA
CBHW030515220526
45464CB00006B/2804